ANOMALY

JAMIE McKENDRICK

Anomaly

FABER & FABER

First published in 2018
by Faber & Faber Ltd
Bloomsbury House
74–77 Great Russell Street
London WC1B 3DA

Typeset by Hamish Ironside
Printed in the UK by TJ International Ltd, Padstow, Cornwall

A CIP record for this book is available from the British Library

ISBN 978-0-571-34921-0

2 4 6 8 10 9 7 5 3 1

Acknowledgements

I'm grateful to the editors of the following magazines and anthologies where some of these poems were first published: *Ash*, *The Arts of Peace*, *Climate of Opinion: Sigmund Freud in Poetry*, *Kathleen Jamie: Poems and Essays on her Work*, *La bella scola: il paradiso terrestre*, *London Review of Books*, *New Statesman*, *Ploughshares*, *Prac Crit*, *Poetry* (Chicago), *Poetry Review*, *Rascal*, *Spectator*, *Subtropics*, *Times Literary Supplement*, *Wild Court* and the *Yellow Nib*.

Incline Press published *The Hunters, Les Chasseurs, Cacciatori* in a limited edition with translations into French and Italian by Gilles Ortlieb and Antonella Anedda. The poem's first line is taken from Thomas Heywood's play *A Woman Killed with Kindness*.

Five of the poems were published in *Repairwork*, a Clutag Press pamphlet.

The quotation in the epigraph for 'Something More' is taken from John Ormsby's 1885 translation of *Don Quixote*. The quotation from Cervantes included in 'A Bad Name' is apocryphal.

In Valerio Magrelli's poem 'Tombeau de Totò', Totò (1898–1967) was the stage name of Antonio De Curtis, a famous Italian comedian, actor and singer.

L'homme qui chavire, known in English as *The Falling Man*, is a sculpture by Alberto Giacometti.

'Capricci of the Lagoon' was commissioned by the Poetry Society & Royal Collection Trust for the Antonio Canaletto exhibition at the Queen's Gallery.

Contents

ANOMALY

The Hunters

We that have been hunting all the day
are mighty tired, our hair is dank with sweat
and by our hunting helmets plastered flat.

As days of hunting go, this must be counted
a good day: the horns blew loud and the dogs
barked hard as though they knew it was more for them

than us we went out hunting the wild beast
all day – so they could teach him just how tame
they were, and how wrong to think that being dogs

had taken the edge off their appetite
for sport. We that have been hunting all the day
will keep on hunting through the night

for finer creatures than the forests hide,
through forests deeper than the ones of day.

Above the Treeline

Up on the alpine rafters, the dragon's spine
that props the bronze pavilion of the sky,
in the thin air only fit for spiders' lungs

I long for the dark wood where I was lost,
for the dog beast and the two big cats
with their earthly instincts and their appetites.

Facing that sky, now far too close,
the church bell deep in the valley sounds
so small it could hang on a cricket's collar.

Anomaly

Never a jay in this neck of the woods
but always the roar of the ring road.

Whiter than clouds the lilac flowers
have now turned a cindery yellow.

Never a chance that you'd hug me again
as you did that once on your doorstep.

Weather worse than last year's came
and felled the tall eucalyptus.

Earscape

Milton lost his sight in libertyes defence
and I my hearing in oyles pursuit employed
by factors who failed to plug our ears with down
I was the fuse-and-dynamite boy who blew
up bits of Derbyshire with blasts that lunged
through the earths crust barrelling out below
to stun the blind mole in its burrow and
bend the funicles of beetles antennae
so now alone or in a crowd I hear
the tinny thrum of protest from the earth
a stridulating bug-eyed orchestra
in the cellar of the battered dandelion
and out in the air beyond our telescopes
the admonition of a blackened star

Back to Black

Hey crow – have you clocked some carrion
or come to make friends. Your croak and cackle's
more tuneful to me than the blatter of grackles,
your black blacker than cormorant or shalik.
Of all the inks I've accrued – the squat bottle
of India pine soot, lampblack and shellac
deepened with a stratum of gum arabic
or Chinese ink stick fine-ground on the ink stone –
none's lacquered and lustrous as yours, none runs
so far from the spectrum or eats the sun
back to a charred bone with quite your sardonic
aplomb. So be a friend and lend me a peck
from your cloak of no colour, your vital and dense,
original virginal evergreen black.

La colonna sonora

has a better ring to it than *soundtrack* –
more vertical, classical, Herculean,
like a pillar of water sustaining a cloud,
a fluted column on a celluloid plinth
that turns our voices into architecture
or, laid on its side like a wooden flute,
a hollow tube with owlish eyes that blink.
When I think of these sonorous columns
the one that wakes in my ear is the wind loud
in the holm oak at the edge of his world
the peasant boy hears in *Padre Padrone*,
the belling sheep, the *cantu a tenòre*,
all the drone and clamour of creation
crushing each creature with the force of nature.

La tempesta

The wicked storm behind the naked woman
swells with whale hide, wolf pelt, stirred concrete,
    kneaded clay,
with blacks of charred vine and vats of tar,
with ash tones, mud hues, iron and heron grey,
which though a mass of vapour reads as solid
as bulbs and beads of hematite. The flood
it holds is for the moment sealed
fast within the anvil of a thunderhead
reared above a broken marble column
some empire left behind when it expired.
As yet no drop of rain has spattered
the tall parched elms and dusky thickets
but it seems the majestic woman still awaits
something more elemental than mere weather.

The Urban Field

Though they've all the rest of the field to graze in
the horses stand at the iron railings by
the main road and philosophically survey
the mode of transport that replaced them.

It seems a silent vigil at their own demise.
Of course it could be they just like the trees
that line the road and act as their
umbrellas, parasols and scratching posts.

Apart from one sleek foal I can't distinguish
young from old – they all seem ageless visitors
from another age. I sit out in the café opposite,

sharing the traffic fumes, and puffing at
this ridiculous 'vapour' cigarette. Feeling my age –
breathless, bereft, my only field the page.

The Altar

Tyne flood, Black Church, Bywell, November 1771

In the great flood that washed away the bridge
  leaving stone stumps adrift and not one arch
  standing, Mr Elliot's mare barged the church
  doors open as the water had already reached
    her heavy hocks. With one bound
    as if to clear the gunwale of the Ark
    she landed on the altar and stood
    not like the sacrificial lamb of God
  but a brazen idol, even if half-drowned.
  She stood that night and the next day too
  until the turbid waters finally withdrew.
Odd that a structure which had been so long of such
dubious usage, for garish ornaments and ghostly food,
should out of the blue become sustaining and rock solid.

Quince

Ignoring the cabbage, the melon and cucumber
– no disrespect meant – I concentrate
on the quince Juan Sánchez Cotán painted
in Naples Yellow, poisonous stuff, mixed with white
judging by the postcard someone sent me
years ago. It hangs on a string, a world to itself,
a quintessence, a quiddity of quince
caught between a jaundiced mortal pallor
and golden life, a hair's breadth, a breath apart.
To eat this thing raw it must be blotched and bletted,
so best boil it down to *dulce de membrillo*
making red jelly out of that hard yellow
– even this size, you feel its density and weight
forged from the steel sunlight of Toledo.

Sequence

THE QUINCE IN FLOWER

And not one love poem?
– I deserve to be alone.

Sent from my iPhone.

TILT

The quince has borne fruit(s)
despite the fox having dug
a hole at its roots.

QUINCITY

Whither, quince, and whence?
Hast withered since? Hailing,
tholing transience.

POISON PALETTE

For quince mix lead-based
Naples Yellow with Flake White.
Curb the urge to taste.

EXILE

after Leonardo Sinisgalli

By now the warm wind
will have come from Salerno
to sweeten the quinces.

Arboreal

Not a trough of adders or a box of hornets
but a tree full of birds was your emblem
of the poet – home for wandering voices

that have no household gods, no roof, no door.
Or if a door an always open door.
Just as Machado valued Virgil not

for his *Eclogues*, *Georgics* or *Aeneid*
but because he's host and haven to
a ghost-guesthood, a close-packed company

of singers, without botching or mangling their notes.
Orchestration – if that weren't such a dud word.
So think of the bird whose head is full of tree,

who sits on the bare branch, guardian of green,
hearing the dim hum of buds in the xylem,
wind rattling her cage of wet, black boughs.

To a Dried-up Elm

Antonio Machado, 'A un olmo seco'

After the rains of April and the suns of May,
the old, blasted elm,
half eaten away,
has just put forth a few green leaves.

The century-old elm up on the hill
past which the Duero flows! Dull
yellow moss badges the whitened bark
on its dusty, carious trunk.

Unlike the song-filled poplars
lining the road and the riverbank,
it won't be the home of nightingales.

Dauntless ants in single file
make their ascent, and in its entrails
spiders drape their drab, grey webs.

Before you fall, elm of the Duero,
to the woodman's axe and the carpenter
planes you down for a church bell's brace,
a carriage axle or the yoke of a cart;
before you redden, tomorrow, in the grate
of some forlorn abode
huddled beside the country road;
before you're torn up by a dust devil
or felled by a gust from the white sierras;
before the river takes you, elm, to the sea
hurtling through valleys and ravines,
I want to preserve, here in my notebook,
the sudden grace of your green-clad branch.

Turned to the light, to the life it might bring,
my heart as much as yours awaits
another miracle of Spring.

A Walk in the Park

A big man like you could surely keep that dog
on a leash my father said – the Commando
chairbound, with swollen legs and wounded feet,
not quite curbing the healthy urge to overbear.

The mad dog, retaining a keen sense of hierarchy,
agreed with a sneer at the underling.
Finally fatherless, no longer the boy
nor, for that matter, the man I was,

I stride out into the open air
and wonder where, after such long deferral,
I'd been meaning to go
off on my own to – perhaps the Palm House

now refurbished for receptions
where we held my mother's wake encircled
by the statues of Mercator, Henry the Navigator,
Darwin, Linnaeus . . . I forget who else – the great
    explorers

bent over their thoughts and charts and quadrants.
A few yards off, the pointless figure of Peter Pan
I've a feeling my mother favoured
looks skyward with a frail air of delight.

He was installed here in 1928 when she was four.
Since then a bronze squirrel was stolen from the base
and some vandal decapitated
an attendant fairy – both now, as things can be,
    restored.

She was born on one side of Sefton Park
and died on the other. To walk – one could do worse –
from Marmion Road to Ibbotson's Lane
might take twenty minutes, or a life.

St Michael-in-the-Hamlet

God it's ugly that church
I have a privileged outlook on
each time I trudge up north
to clock in for the ministry
of my pinched quota of care,
but ugly falls a notch short of
its dank brick and dead salmon
colour scheme, its fat jaggedly
tapering square tower topped
with oversized fake Gothic finials
in the same unappetising
marzipannish pink that graces
the stretched ogives of its rusted
iron windows, windows missing
a few lozenges of clear glass
and ending in ventilation slats
embodged with pigeon cack.
Completed between the eruption
of Mount Tambora and
the Battle of Waterloo,
it seems to have been finished
in bloodstained lava,
and sports a skeleton of cast iron –
trademark of the builder John Cragg
who owned the Mersey Iron Foundry
and built the house I write in,
wielding weight and welding
clumpish structures skyward.
Maybe God doesn't give a damn
for churches, or good taste,
which is not to say

He doesn't have any.
He might prefer a simple heart,
a wasp's nest or a lean-to shed
to this dreary steeple house
that somehow fluked a Grade
I listing. But ugly as this church
most surely is, it's still,
worse luck, more home to me
than any mosque or duomo
in peerless travertine or marble,
though I've other things to care about
than this, such as doling out tablets
or emptying a bottle of piss
left beside the threadbare throne
my father's realm has shrunk to,
before my name is boomed out once again
in his still undiminished bass.
The cloud of darkness
that's been gathering for months
slowly leaves his face
as he tells me of the German colonel
who'd gone scouting too close to
the English line, near Bremen,
and was blown up by a shell.
The Worcesters found him lying
on his side with multiple
fractures to all four limbs.
'Hilfe' was all he said
'fünf Tage und nichts zu trinken.'
My father patched him up
as best he could and always
wondered if he made it,
the only German he'd felt sorry for.
In the night he shouts for my sister,
demands she call an ambulance

this minute, can't she see
the colonel's dying, he points to the floor,
it's a bloody disgrace
to leave him lying there.

Tombeau de Totò

Valerio Magrelli, 'Tombeau de Totò'

As an old man, Totò became blind.
All that rubber-limbed gallivanting
just to end up in the dark.
A tentative groping,
a zigzag through darkness.
But the opposite is also true.
As a blind man, he became old.
I still remember him, nearby my house,
crossing the street for a funeral,
between two wings of a cheering crowd.
And he was playing along, disjointed, moving jerkily,
without seeing anything – that, I've only just
    understood!
Blind, old and mechanical,
but wound up by the steel spring of his Neapolitan
    dialect.

At least until, having lost his sight, he also lost
    his speech.
In his last films, unable to say his lines,
he had to be dubbed. The story goes
that having gone blind he then went dumb
during the shoot, so another voice
had to stand in for his own.
Blasphemous Totò-fakery. On the verge of darkness.

Vision extinguished, speech annulled,
the ragtag body descends into the grave.

Hibernaculum

*'Hibernaculum' is his [Gilbert White's] word for the winter
quarters a swallow repairs to, but where was this hibernaculum?*
    – KATHLEEN JAMIE, *Sightlines*

I am here with the swallows that failed to migrate,
resting up, oiling my wings. Here, in case
you'd like to know, wherever you've intrepidly
flown off south to, hasn't an actual address –
there isn't much sun, or much anything
and the cold makes my head-magnet ache,
or is it a clock the creator implanted
to make our departures so effortlessly punctual?
I've been keeping bad time, and losing my way.

With impairment, I'm not ourself: I is
another – famous phrase of one hirondelle
who risked a solo flight to Africa
and only made it back when truly crippled,
scorched and songless. All that came
so naturally is now you've no idea
how much of an effort, but still
this cavern is like a pale blue crystal
magnifying the little light that remains.

Truth is, as you can see, my imagination
is suffering from a dearth of the facts yours
is always nourished by as you fly
into the clean north wind or alight
on a TV aerial, the edge of a townland.
On bad days, it's more like a hospital here
– with the staff and caterers out on strike –
than any kind of splendid winter residence,
but despite the dark, the long nights and this

particular winter's refusal to end;
despite the depleted store of tawny grubs
and the dull vexations I should have shed,
but just to give you one example:
some spotty fledgling in the *Avian Times*
calls my song 'awkward' and 'uninspired' – well
you should listen to *his* twittery scritchings;
despite the dark days and the splitting nights
I intend to hold out till your return.

The Flight

Others look down on me. As well they might.
I look down on myself from a great height:
see the tramp's straggly hair turned white

– the off-white of effluent-polluted sea-foam –
the bony shoulders, the incipient bald dome
and black wings sprouting that will fly me home.

L'homme qui chavire

The falling man – if that makes sense – is falling
into a void he has failed to avoid,
a nothing nothing has prepared him for,
and the air, the vagrant air, that served
to hold him up has taken flight
to uphold something else, elsewhere.
His own two feet on which he used to stand
have lost their foothold: *pieds-sans-terre*.
The axis that aligned his thighbones
with his pelvis and his spine is
a capsized keystone and a veering steeple,
– a sad jumble of anatomy who knows
what witchy pins or poultices can couple.

Reprieve

That splintered bones can mend might give us hope
time's arrow doesn't always have to rush
thoughtlessly forward but can choose to stop
mid-air, mid-flight, look round about then step
aside or even back, hold up the cortège
that's winding through the suburbs in the wake
of the redhead who wears an inappropriate
short black dress and swings a swagger stick
out of time with the angelic oboes
whose scattered notes make buried bones so light.

Questionnaire on Matters Physical and Metaphysical

What is the insect known as Rama's arrow
(that along with the termites ingested
so many ancient Tamil poems writ
on palm leaves in the curvilinear script
which may well have evolved so as not to split
the brittle fibres)? And what was Rama's arrow
originally (and through how many aeons
did it fly with its barely rippling crow
feathers and flexing shaft, and then through what
fields of night and yawning space before
returning to contrive the end of days)?
And the end of days is the beginning of what
(turbulent timeless tract where all of space
does or does not collapse into a witless dot)?

Repairwork

for Amit Chaudhuri

And this my hand, against my self uprear . . .
– WILLIAM SHAKESPEARE, Sonnet XLIX

I took the crooked, arcade-overshadowed road
off the main square built by De Chirico
and chanced upon a watch repairer's shop
which might have been painted by Bhupen Khakhar
for whose summer show the London weeklies
have just prepared such a frosty welcome.
Wait. Is this ekphrastic or oneiric?
The site Bologna or Bombay?
Are the hanging watches, so sure of their gender,
Bulgari or Janata? Too early to tell.
But there he sat at his workbench working at

what looked like tiny jewelled bits of time laid out
under his eye loupe in magnolia light.
These fragments he seemed to be reassembling
into a perfect circle, or a sphere seen from above –
it was like a miracle obligingly performed
in slow motion, or the flight of an arrow broken down
into ever smaller fractions of advancement.
He took his time, and my time, to acknowledge me –
clearly he didn't crave an audience
as though the slow work that so ravished him
required if not secrecy at least discretion.

Could he mend, I wondered, the cracked glass
on my watch before I had to leave tomorrow?
His black eyes rested on the old Omega
as though bemused such a watch should belong

to someone so importunate, then he cleared the air
with a lenient, experienced smile.
Certo. But it will have a different *bombatura*
not quite as fine as this one was.
Though the word was unfamiliar, it conjured up at once
light skating the rim of a sheer bevel.
Va bene. So long, I thought, as I can tell

the time, and don't have to squint through cracks
as I had since fending off a drunken punch
which I'd provoked myself enough to throw.
I would have paid extra to watch him clean the face
with the wad of turquoise putty he had to hand,
paid double to have Devanagari numerals
replace the Roman, but he wanted me out.
A domani allora. Then as I left
he said it needed *una revisione completa*
before it got too late. A watch like this deserves
– he changed the tense – deserved a lot more care.

Very Fine Fake

It's too late to ask my father now
where in Athens and from which
wily trader he bought the two fake coins –
the silver 'owl' stater, circa 270 BC,
for himself, and the tetradrachm for me –
with his unerring gift to sniff out
a hopeless deal, and clinch it. Now the forgery's
exposed and the auction house has regretfully
returned them, I'm glad they're back and that
the stater fooled one sharp-eyed, in-house expert.
On the Paul Menard principle
they're finer than originals could be
– how much more work and ingenuity,
more art and subtle plotting it cost
to forge them more than two millennia later
than just hammer out run-of-the-mill
coinage for mere commodities,
for goats and cabbages and olive oil.
Up in my loft, walled in with worthless paper,
I shall turn them in the light,
with their two blinking owls,
and savour the wisdom of the counterfeit.

Translating Yves Bonnefoy

for Stephen Romer

I was eating alone in Arezzo
eavesdropping on the conversation of Yves
Bonnefoy who happened to be at the next table

with his Italian translator. My hearing, hélas, is bad
as my French, my memory hardly better –
which made me far from fit to profit

from this chance the muses or the maître d'
had served me up with. I had little doubt
I was in the presence of greatness –

his age impressive, and his face
forged by the thyme-scented air of the midi.
I tried to shush the chewing for that, as only

the deaf know, plays havoc with the ears.
Someone, the poet said, had *un menton immense*
– almost the start of a poem . . . it reminded me

of Joyce's sentence: 'Maria had a very long nose
and a very long chin, and when she smiled they
almost met.' (In all likelihood, a misquote.)

The word *voiture* alerted me to a change of tack:
je n'ai pas le permis . . . being driven by his wife
was either a boon or a curse, I couldn't hear which.

Much droll detail followed, lost on me,
but I could take or leave his views on cars
for it's not a topic poets excel on –

and even if I haven't made one, I've driven
from Naples to Liverpool and back again,
and spent hours after spare parts in oily dumps.

However, in a lower, shielded tone,
during their next course, he spoke of
la parole . . . la poésie du concept . . . la réalité . . .
  le cinéma . . .

This was the stuff I most needed to catch.
Having read his Rimbaud book when just
out of my teens, and not finding there what I was

earnestly looking for, now the lost gold might
belatedly surface and all my confusions
be resolved. But no such luck – I began

to feel uneasy like Gene Hackman
in *The Conversation*, only without
his directional zoom microphones.

Another clear phrase formed which I translated as
'Americans speak English' but it might have been
'the English Americans speak', the first almost

incontrovertible, the second needing some development
really to qualify as wisdom, such as 'the English
Americans speak is richer and stranger than the English

the English speak'. If so I would willingly speak
American, speak to myself that is, in the perfect accent
I almost always achieve when no one's listening.

I could not fault Yves Bonnefoy's French accent.
It was marvellous, liquid, like a native speaker's,
only he received relatively low marks

for audibility – he was clearly indifferent
to his extended audience, and I can't help feeling
that counts against him. Perhaps you'll say

I ought to read his poems. Well, doubtless I should.
In the meantime, though, I'd be none the wiser,
so I returned to my own heavy thoughts and my plate

of earthy beans and bitter chicory.

Il gran rifiuto

In the sacred wood
wrought poems hang
well within reach
on every branch,

all rounded, golden,
almost flawless –
the least would earn
eternal fame.

But where's the buzz
in a gift without graft?
Like Jonson's eels
that leap into your hand.

I turned on my heel
and left the place
for the stony field
I plough in vain.

A Bad Name

Months had passed without a single word to greet my latest production. Then one morning, in a national newspaper, I saw with relief the title of my book. But where the author's name should be I read in astonishment *Slackmore Snagglebooth*. After some sly merriment at the expense of the name, that I now realised was bound to stick, the reviewer became serious: 'We could wish Snagglebooth some adversity in his future, as on the evidence of this work little seems to have ruffled his affluent composure . . .' Well thanks for that – a hex on top of a hatchet job.

When my companion read the piece she gave a discreet chuckle, then seeing my expression, she straightened her mouth and said 'When the dogs bark, that means you're really moving.' Apparently something from Cervantes. She explained that those were Sancho Panza's words of encouragement to Don Quixote. If she remembered right, it was when the Don was galloping away at what he took to be breakneck speed, mounted on the clap-board flanks of a rocking horse.

Freudiana

I. ILL

. . . we are all ill, i.e. neurotic . . .
– SIGMUND FREUD

All ill, some very, some not so much or not
so evidently – though perhaps for that
all the more ill. Overall I'd say I was ill,
but not quite ill all over as there's still
some small patch of well, a window sill
of the psyche I can look out from
and see how much more ill you are than I am.

II. ROYAL

Dreams are the royal road to the unconscious.
— SIGMUND FREUD

A royal road, a ragged road,
a ruffian, raffish, rascal road,
I dreamt a road the royals ran
between their various castles and
the barracks where their guards abode.
We run this road the royals roared
because this road is ours not yours,
it's ours because it was decreed
this road be called the royal road.
It wasn't called the public street
nor was it called the common way;
it wasn't paved for common feet,
and if you want to pass you pay
with coins whose heads are royal heads,
whose tails wear plumes of royalty.
The road was ours since time began
and time is also ours not yours,
for as we hardly need to say
it was decreed that hours should be,
that hours and years and eras be
prerogatives of royalty.

The Long Haul

The heart is young, but the heels are leaden.
– R. L. STEVENSON, *The Story of a Lie*

The way I'm going these Spanish boots,
waiting for their owner to catch up,
may well outlast me – last is what they'll do,
with their straps and buckles and rubber soles

cut out of lorry tyres that still preserve
a slight curvature from the many roads they once
lugged their freight along, curled up
against the earth's circumference.

The heels a wee bit shauchled but the treads still sharp,
ten years of wear have barely worn them down –
years their wearer's borne with less élan.
The way I'm going these soles have gone before

bearing a far more heavy load
from Al-Ándalus to the Ampurdán,
where a cobbler stitched them to the leather uppers,
though someone since has filled these heels with lead.

Something More

Thou must take notice, brother Sancho, that this adventure and those like it are not adventures of islands, but of cross-roads, in which nothing is got except a broken head and an ear the less: have patience, for adventures will present themselves from which I may make you not only a governor but something more.
                                       – CERVANTES, *Don Quixote*

We could have lived quite well on Sancho's island,
his governance more competent than ours.
There'd be a welcome party on the strand
for the rafts of Indians, Moriscos, Moors.

But now we must abide at cross-roads,
under a sad flag, awaiting adventures,
with the eternal promise of 'something more'.
A stove-in helmet, a half-severed ear,
and the dust of a mule track our only reward.

The Dirt-Painter

*Pyreicus, who painted barbers' rooms, dirty workshops,
donkeys, and kitchen herbs, with all the diligence of a Dutch
painter, as if such things were rare or attractive in nature,
acquired the surname of Rhyparographer, the dirt-painter.*
          – GOTTHOLD EPHRAIM LESSING, *Laocoon*

While the rest were slavering over Gods and heroes
we favoured his paintings of the blacksmith's forge,
rat tails of cut hair or tufts of grey sage,
the donkey forlorn in its scabby meadow.

Spurning the strained postures of the muscle-bound,
he found a palette for the glaucous sporangia
of moss, for the faintest stain on the air,
and turned all background into foreground.

Lives of the Artists

And then there was the swaggering Daimon
who went about in Tyrian purple
and wore a white fillet on his oiled head
while boasting of his humble heritage.
His masterwork was a golden skull
studded with diamonds. That winning touch,
much valued by his patron, the wife-throttler Sātchios,
involved a trick a shade less effortful
than Midas's, for all he managed
was to turn gold into gold, and flesh to cash.

Cartoline

for Rachel Owen

1.

I keep forgetting if this is
Lucerne or Geneva, Geneva or Lucerne.
But there's a lake almost too close
like a slab of black marble.
Every hour a ferry slides over and erases
its lucid inscriptions.

2.

In Tarragona you can swim a few strides
from the port road – it looks clean enough
to drown in, but it takes a bloody cliff
to reach the Rambla Vella and the Roman ruins.
I opt for a dip in the drink.
Why scale the heights when you can fight the waves?

3.

Free passage to Cagliari, that's if
I can speak about the First World War
poets. I speak too much. Break of day,
a trench for sewage pipes is being dug
outside the hotel window. Hard hats are
placidly conferring. A Phoenician frigate in the port.

4.

The interminable cave through the Karst
 – the White War fought in the near distance –
is home to the blind salamander and the devil bat.
They say Dante in exile visited and first
dreamt up hell down here – they forget
he spent his youth in Florence.

Annales

Antonella Anedda, 'Annales'

Rereading Tacitus during this summer of massacres
there was some solace to be had from the Latin, the
    bareness
of facts, the near absence of adjectives, the use of
    gerunds
to avoid futile repetitions. If you compared the Italian
    translation
with the original, the text was longer, the blood
    poured more slowly
between the lines. In days filled with banners raised
    in various
battle lines, the syntax worked like a blood drip,
contracted the emotions, acted like a barrier to tears.
Sestilia, mother of the Vitelli – ancient Moors – never
    exulted,
Tacitus recounts, over her fortune, but felt only her
    family's griefs.
Tacitus's grey book written when he was sixty
tells only what it must. On the grey horizon of the
    Annals
there's no room for landscape or for love.
How else to tell the woes of these wars?
– 'The rooted greed of mortals, the reward
for informers no less dire than for culprits,
the iron of weapons ratifying gold.'

Trauma

I'm reminded of another episode in my life concerning bees. A trauma, certainly. I was taking the air when with two blunt taps first one, then another bee flew into the centre of my forehead, more or less where the third eye is meant to look out. Both bees fell stunned onto the pavement where they writhed as if trying to free themselves from an invisible spider's web. I was conversant enough with common bee-lore to know that in the normal course of events this meant a warning; that to proceed would be to risk the ire of the hive; and that the best course was to retrace my steps backwards. But this proved not to be in the normal course, for I observed that the pavement was strewn with bees in a similar state of extreme distress. Some, it seemed, had already died and lay curled up like vacant, furry shells. I followed the trail of them, careful where I trod, to a house with an open door from which issued a cloud of cement. I tried to explain to the workmen inside that it didn't have to be an either/or as regards human and bee residence, that we could both live together to our mutual and happy advantage. To this they listened sympathetically for a few minutes, then explained that although they could see what I was saying they had a lot of work to finish. When I protested, they chased me away with shovels, shouting that I was a traitor and a disgrace.

Hearing Voices

He began to hear voices in early April, though the month and the changeable weather barely impinged on their matter. They said things pointedly but not vehemently, things of which the context remained obscure such as 'it's not an especially distinguished name in Norwegian', or 'do you have any more chipmunk tokens?', or 'the car with a quiff looks better parked', or 'they should mend the hut before the green arrives'. Perhaps not voices but merely a single voice cut off as abruptly as it began. It was as if he was only hearing one clear part sheared from the middle of an exchange, something overheard on a train or in a queue, just to the left of him and slightly behind, yet he would be alone at the time and slumped on a chair that used to swivel. If he weren't such a slow thinker he might one day be allowed to enter the conversation.

The Ghost

Charles Baudelaire, 'Le revenant'

Like an angel with predatory eyes
I'll be back – back at your bedside,
so sleek you'll hardly hear me glide
cloaked in night's shadows.

I'll plant my moon-cold kisses
across your black satin skin.
You'll feel the chill of my caresses
like a serpent's coils tightening.

When dingy daylight reappears,
you'll find my place empty,
the sheets without a trace or crease.

Others may try tenderness
to curb your youth and beauty,
but me, I mean to rule by fear.

The River Bo

Aldo Palazzeschi, 'Il rio Bo'

Three little sheds
with pointy roofs,
a wee meadow
and this meagre brook – the River Bo.
And don't forget the lordly cypress.
A tiny hamlet, I'm bound to admit,
a nothing of a place, and yet
there's always a star up above,
a magnificent great big star
that would gladden the most depressed . . .
It lines up with the very tip
of the cypress
that rears at the verge of
the exiguous River Bo.
Is that star in love?
It might well be so
as even the biggest city hasn't got
such a thing to boast of.

Capricci of the Lagoon

In Canaletto's canvases the eye, that sleek
conveyance, travels down watery corridors
like a gondola on wheels
whose rims barely scratch
the glassy surface.

*

This *Capriccio* shows a giant urn
carried from the isle of shades
on the crest of a green wave
across the lagoon and past
the oligarchs' megayachts.

*

My third Biennale – to cruise once more
through a glut of money and art . . . almost reconciles me
to petty, internecine poetry.
Compaesano! The Neapolitan bouncer
lets me gatecrash the British Council party.

*

Behind splendour, ruination.
Behind the lion's tawny paws
on an azure ground
the humble rat. Behind
the crimson procession, the plague.

*

(Sorry. I have to stop things there.
My rat's not Eliot's vile Rialto slur.
Nor even Rosenberg's parleying, droll rat.
But simply *Rattus rattus*, ratty rat,
of pestilent bacilli, the innocent vector.)

*

Fine to pretend an impossible
vista exists, to bend
the actual field of the eye
to include the ideal
but when does an inch become a mile?

*

Did the light go out for Canaletto
when, following the money, he came to London?
One contemporary British critic
deemed him an impostor. Be that as it may,
if it were now he'd be a bargaining chip.

*

'The sands of Venice never sunk
under the weight of a war tower; and her roof terraces
were wreathed with Arabian imagery, of golden globes
suspended on the leaves of lilies'
– Ruskin's resonant prose chopped up (one 'of' per line).

*

Girt with ropes and pulleys, San Marco's campanile
has a long jagged edge in this ink sketch
– a rare relief amid all the ruled lines
but the result of lightning, so it counts
more as God's than Canaletto's handiwork.

*

On Elide's roof garden in I forget which *rione*
we sipped some pink drink and watched San Simeone's
green peaked dome inflate then float off
towards the mainland where it clipped the top
of a Mestre oil refinery chimney.

*

Canaletto constructed in oil and coarse-weave canvas
Palladio's impractical Rialto bridge
so sturdily that boats can still pass
under its echoing triple arch
and visitors take selfies in its cool arcade.

*

Underneath the Giants' Stairway
leading, in two flights, to the Ducal Palace
lies a narrow dungeon reserved for traitors.
All day they feel the steps of the ambassadors,
all night the weight of Neptune and Mars.

Twinned

STORRINGTON

Place of storks and green-
clad chalk. Are the Gypsies still
perched on 'The Warren'?

CAMARGUE

Flamingo heaven,
white horses, black madonna.
Heart's grey forgiven.

CAMARGUE

Red dust on the shoes
of Gaditans carrying
Sara-la-Kali.

STORRINGTON

At the age of eight:
the camp fire by their wagon
shed heavenly light.

The Bluff

The newt that plays so delicately dead
must be on the qui vive unless terror
just flicks the switch. Its limbs go limp,
its upturned orange underbelly over-ripe:
a toxic flag unfurled from the beyond.
– Clubbed fingers, clammy-green and spectral,
appear to have slipped off the frets
of a miniature guitar.

Unstrung, inert, the major risk it runs
from a sentimental species such as ours
is premature burial, but even that it seems to have
rehearsed for, lying days out under a stone.
It keeps dead up for quite some time and then
gives itself away. A blink. A twitch. How easily
it shuffles off its life – and then its death.

If this is play, it's play for mortal stakes.
Play for keeps and not keepsakes.
An all-in bluff no river card could save.
Sorry to intrude, I replace the newt
beneath its stone. There it can lie
pretending, presumably, to be alive.